LIFE SUPPORTS

Just skim to enact

BLS
BASIC LIFE
SUPPORT

Niranjan Wadekar BSN
Registered Nurse & First Aid Instructor
Just Udo Aviation Pvt Ltd (FLY91), Headquarters
Ribandar, North Goa
Goa, India

CONTENTS

Foreword

As we embark on the journey of exploring the intricate world of life support, we are reminded of the profound impact our work has on the lives of those in need. The realm of life support technology is a testament to the remarkable advancements in medical science and the unwavering dedication of healthcare professionals like you.

In this book, we delve into the complexities and nuances of life support, recognizing the critical role it plays in providing essential care and support to patients in their most vulnerable moments. Through our collective knowledge, expertise, and compassion, we strive to uphold the highest standards of care and ensure the well-being of those entrusted to our care.

As we navigate the challenges and opportunities that come with the practice of life support, let us remain steadfast in our commitment to excellence, empathy, and continuous learning. Together, we can make a difference in the lives of our patients and their families, offering hope, comfort, and healing in times of need.

Thank you for your dedication, your passion, and your unwavering commitment to the noble profession of medicine and nursing. May this book serve as a valuable resource and guide as we continue to advance the field of life support and enhance the quality of care for all those we serve.

I confidence, this test book will appeal to a wide audience within the medical profession and is to be recommended in any medical and nursing library portfolio.

Dr.Ashok Kamat
Professor
Department of Nursing Foundation
KAHER Institute of Nursing Sciences, Belagavi, Karnataka

Foreword

Aviation professional and founder owner of aviation companies, I found Mr Wadekar very much passionate about human wellbeing and He is always ready to help the needy during their need. I have gone through the recent book authored by Mr Wadekar and I must say that his dedication and knowledge in the field of medical is recommendable, especially he is much aware of aviation medical emergencies, life support system during flight which is crucial part in aviation/aerospace industry.

He has beautifully delivered the articles & way of handling the emergency situations in his book that can be easily understood by a common human being.

I am sure that the contribution by Mr Wadekar will help society in a much easier way.

I wish Mr Wadekar all the best for his future endeavors and more success in the coming years.

Mr Satendra Deshik Sharma
Founder, Owner
Pinakshakti Aerospace Pvt Ltd
Ayanara Aviation Services LLP
Pinakshakti Flapone Aviation Pvt Ltd
Contrails Consultant LLP
APASA, The Food Station Pvt Ltd

Foreword

It is my absolute pleasure to give my sincere feedback for 'Life Supports'. The author has joined the field of Aviation and I have been in Aviation for 27 years. First Aid is a mandatory subject for all crew in aviation and I have gone through this mandatory training on multiple occasions.

The simple manner in which any person can respond in the case of a cardiac arrest and potentially save a human life has been explained in a very lucid manner. This book has the potential to save life and therefore is priceless when the learnings are applied.

I wish the Author all the best for his stupendous effort.

Capt. Amardeep Singh Sarai
Chief of Flight Safety
Just Udo Aviation Pvt Ltd (FLY91), Headquarters, Goa

Preface

As a nurse by profession, I began my career by endeavouring to focus on life while overcoming obstacles. After being hired by a well-known healthcare organization to get experience, my nerves pushed me into the industrial sector, where I currently work; In addition to advancing my career with a variety of new skills and expertise.

The journey of witnessing life lost due to a few failures to recognize the critical role, first responders play in the emergency situation served as the inspiration for this book. This book is based on real-world scenarios that show what happens in an emergency and how we, as lay person or healthcare professionals, can handle casualties at the first point of contact.

The book "LIFE SUPPORTS" is divided into chapters that cover a variety of crucial subjects in a way that is simple enough for a layperson to understand and apply in an emergency.

Niranjan Wadekar
22 May 2024

Acknowledgment

I would submit at the feet of the Universal Creator for the world's well-being and the accomplishment of all my endeavours'.

I would like to take this opportunity to publicly thank Notion Press, for their invaluable assistance in bringing a long-discussed concept to paper.

I am grateful to the Department of Nursing Foundation at KAHER Institute of Nursing Sciences, Belagavi, for their assistance and guidance during my academic career. They have provided me with intriguing knowledge at the ground level, practical skills that have been verified, and an authoritative theoretical background.

I extend my thank feelings to:

Dr Ashok Kamat, for agreeing to write the book's foreword as well as for his insightful advice and outstanding assistance.

Capt Amardeep Singh Sarai, for his extraordinary help, which included taking the time to peruse my book and contributing his opinions to script the foreword.

Mr Satendra Deshik Sharma, for your prompt recognition and support. Furthermore, I appreciate the insightful remarks he made through an excellent Foreword.

Mr Virupaxappa Savadi, for your unflinching encouragement, support and guidance along my life's journey.

My sincere gratitude to my parents, Mr. Rajakumar Wadekar and Mrs. Seema R. Wadekar, for their unwavering support, positive reinforcement, and direction, which has strengthened my determination to release this work of art.

ABBREVIATIONS

A	
ABCD	Airway, Breathing, Circulation, Differential Diagnosis
ACE	Angiotensin-converting Enzyme
ACLS	Advanced Cardiovascular Life Support
ACS	Acute Coronary Syndromes
AED	Automated External Defibrillator
AHF	Acute Heart Failure
AIVR	Accelerated Idioventricular Rhythm
AMI	Acute Myocardial Infarction
aPTT	Activated Partial Thromboplastin Time
AP	Anteroposterior
B	
BLS	Basic Life Support [Check Responsiveness, activate emergency response system, check carotid pulse, provide defibrillation]
C	
CARES	Cardiac Arrest Registry to Enhance Survival
CPR	Cardiopulmonary Resuscitation
CPSS	Cincinnati Prehospital Stroke Scale
CT	Computed Tomography
CCF	Chest Compression Fraction
D	
DNAR	Do Not Attempt Resuscitation
E	
ECG	Electrocardiogram
ED	Emergency Department
EMS	Emergency Medical Services
ET	Endotracheal
F	
FDA	Food and Drug Administration
FiO2	Fraction of Inspired Oxygen

G	
GI	Gastrointestinal

I	
ICU	Intensive Care Unit
INR	International Normalised Ratio
IO	Intraosseous
IV	Intravenous

L	
LMWH	Low-molecular-weight Heparin
LV	Left ventricle / Left ventricular
LUD	Lateral Uterine Displacement

M	
mA	Milliamperes
MACE	Major adverse cardiac events
MI	Myocardial Infarction
mm Hg	Millimetres of mercury

N	
NIH	National Institutes of Health
NIHSS	National Institutes of Health Stroke Scale
NINDS	National Institutes of Neurological Disorders and Stroke
NPA	Nasopharyngeal Airway
NSAIDs	Nonsteroidal anti-inflammatory drugs
NSTEMI	Non-ST-segment elevation Myocardial Infarction

O	
OPA	Oropharyngeal airway

P	
$PaCO_2$	Partial pressure of CO_2 in arterial blood
PCI	Percutaneous Coronary Intervention
PE	Pulmonary Embolism
PEA	Pulseless Electrical Activity
PT	Prothrombin Time
PAD	Public Access Defibrillation
pVT	Pulseless Ventricular Tachycardia

R	
ROSC	Return of Spontaneous Circulation
RRT	Rapid Response Team
rtPA	Recombinant tissue plasminogen activator
RV	Right ventricle / Right ventricular
S	
SBP	Systolic Blood Pressure
STEMI	ST-segment elevation Myocardial Infarction
SVT	Supraventricular Tachycardia
T	
TCP	Transcutaneous pacing
TVP	Transvenous pacing
T-CPR	Telecommunicator assisted - CPR
U	
UA	Unstable Angina
UFH	Unfractionated heparin
V	
VF	Ventricular fibrillation
VT	Ventricular tachycardia

CHAPTER 1
INTRODUCTION

BLS

BLS in general, describes the kind of care that emergency medical personnel, first responders or public safety specialists give to anyone who is having a cardiac arrest, an obstruction in their airway or respiratory distress [1].

IMPORTANCE OF TO WHY UNDERGO BLS TRAINING

Those who accomplish BLS training can potentially save the life of an unconscious person who is not breathing. It will be up to first responders like you to save lives during these potentially fatal situations [2].

MAIN COMPONENTS OF CPR

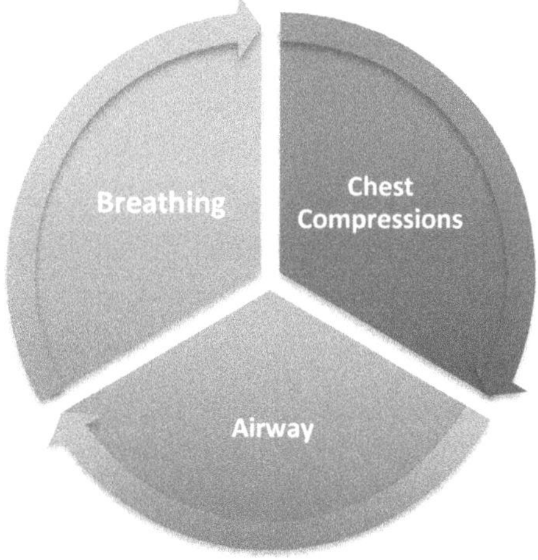

HIGH QUALITY CPR INDEX

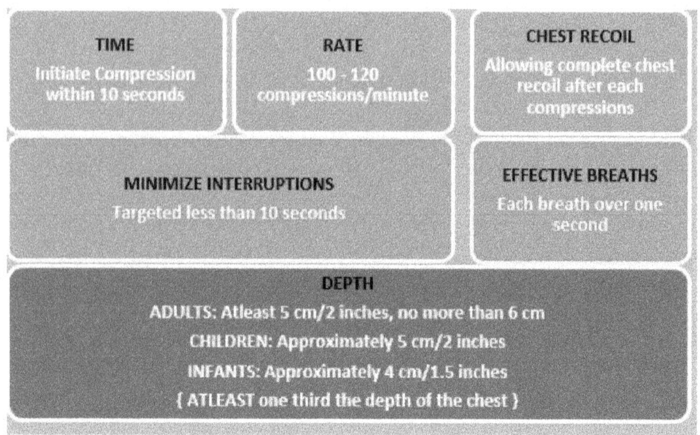

AGE CATEGORIES

INFANTS: 28 days to 12 months/1 year.
CHILDREN: 1 year to puberty (Male: Hairs on chest and underarm, Female: Any Breast development).
ADULT: Signs of puberty and above [3].

CHAIN OF SURVIVAL

1) Adult Out-of-hospital:

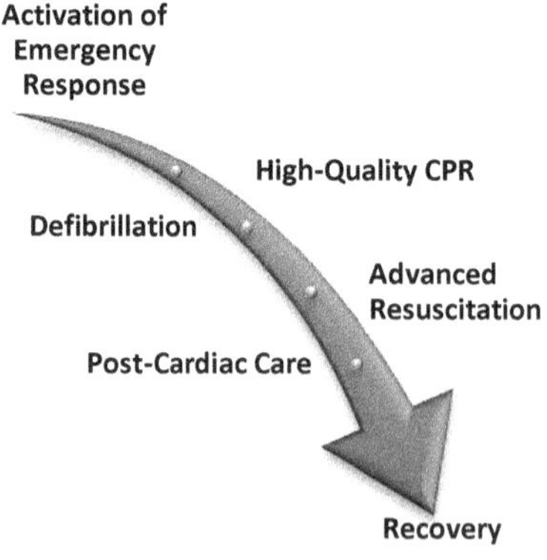

2) Adult In-hospital:

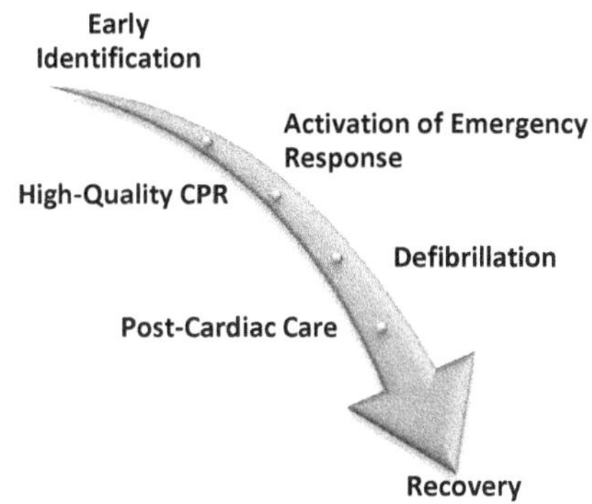

3) Paediatric Out-of-hospital:

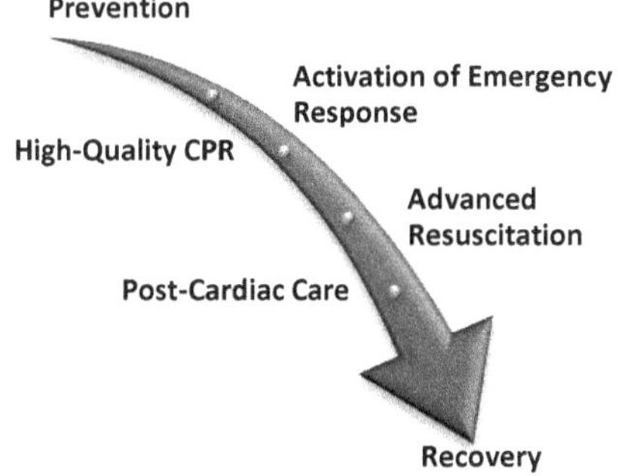

4) Paediatric In-hospital:

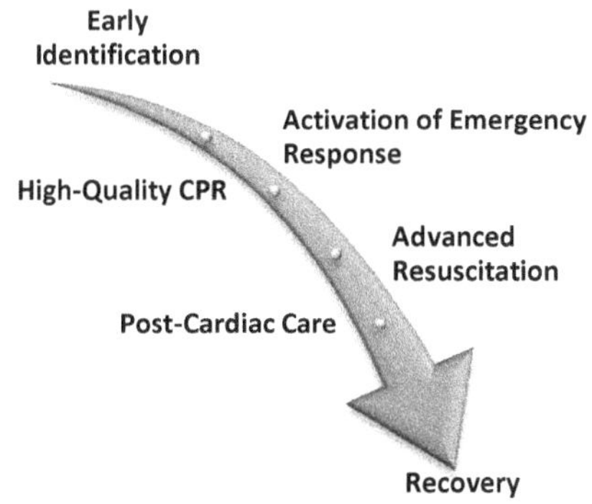

COMPARISON OF CHAIN OF SURVIVAL [4]

Step	Layperson not trained	Trained layperson	Healthcare Professional
1	Check whether surrounding is safe.	Check whether surrounding is safe	Check whether surrounding is safe
2	Check for victim's response.	Check for victim's response.	Check for victim's response.
3	Shout for help or ask someone to activate emergency response system or call ambulance.	Shout for help or ask someone to activate emergency response system or call ambulance.	Shout for help or ask someone to activate emergency response system or call ambulance.
4	Follow the on-call instructions.	Check for breathing & pulse. If no breathing or only gasping; then provide rescue breaths. If none, begin CPR with chest compressions.	Check for breathing & pulse. If no breathing or only gasping; then provide rescue breaths. If none, begin CPR with chest compressions. Ask someone to bring AED. On arrival connect AED and after delivering shock resume CPR until advance help arrives.
5	Look for no breathing or only gasping, at the direction on-call.	Answer the on-call questions and follow the instructions.	Immediately begin CPR and use the AED/defibrillator when available.
6	Follow the on-call instructions.	Send the second person to retrieve an AED, if one is available.	When the second rescuer arrives, provide 2-rescuer CPR and use the AED/defibrillator.

KEY DETAILS FROM CHAIN OF SURVIVAL

<u>ADULT:</u> Cardiac Arrest is often sudden and frequent.
<u>CHILDREN:</u> Cardiac Arrest is often secondary to respiratory failure.

PERSONAL PROTECTIVE EQUIPMENT

Gloves, Gowns and Aprons, Face masks, Respirators, Goggles and Face shield [5].

CHAPTER 2
BLS FOR ADULTS

HIGH-QUALITY CPR COMPONENTS

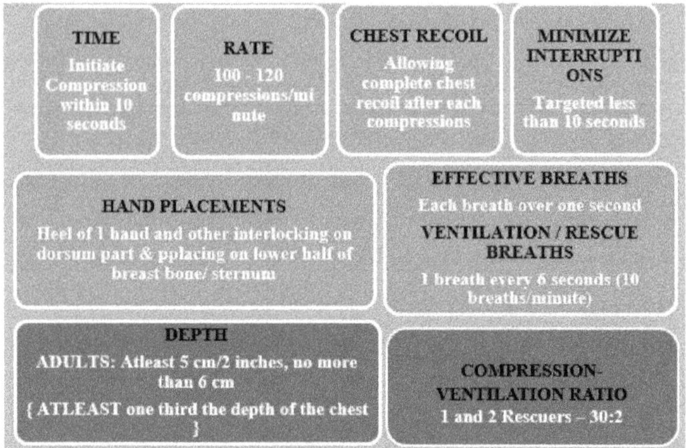

HIGH QUALITY CPR SKILLS: ADULTS

> AGONAL GASPING, ARE NOT NORMAL BREATHS
> (These are initial signs present post cardiac arrest)

1) <u>BREATHING:</u>

1) Check for chest rise and fall.
2) Victim's breathing: Monitor until advance help arrives.
3) Victim isn't breathing: Get ready for High-quality CPR.

2) <u>PULSE CHECK:</u>

SITE: Carotid pulse.
1) Assess for victim's Trachea, using index and middle finger onto your side.
2) Slightly downward between the trachea and muscles of neck, you can feel carotid pulse.

CHEST COMPRESSIONS

Until the heart can be shocked, chest compressions help restore blood flow to the brain and other essential organs, such as the lungs and the heart itself [6].

1) <u>POSITION:</u>

Supine position, on victim's back, flat surface.

2) <u>INTERRUPTIONS:</u>

Lesser the interruptions = Best the outcome.

The ratio of the overall amount of time spent during chest compression to the cumulative time spent for entire resuscitation.

$$CCF = \frac{\text{Total time spent on chest compressions}}{\text{Overall time spent for resuscitation}} * 100$$

At least 60% increase likelihood of survival of ROSC, A good teamwork can achieve 80% survival [7].

3) <u>COMPRESSIONS IN PREGNANT WOMEN:</u>

Left uterine displacement needs to be done during resuscitation in order to stop preload reductions as it is more difficult to achieve the proper compression force. Manual left uterine displacement can be carried out from the patient's right side by pushing the uterus up and to the left, or from the patient's left side by pulling the uterus upward and to the left with two hands [8].

PROVIDING BREATHS

Methods of opening airway:

1) <u>HEAD TILT- CHIN LIFT:</u>

1) Placing one hand on victim's forehead and push palm to tilt head back.
2) Placing the other hand fingers below the bony part of chin and lifting it forward.

2) <u>JAW THURST</u>:

This technique is used when the victim has spine, neck injury.
1) Positioning yourself at victim's head end side.
2) Place each of hands on each side of victim's face, and your fingers under the victim's lower jaw and lifting both hands results the jaw forward.

BARRIER DEVICES FOR PROVIDING BREATHS

1) <u>POCKET MASK</u>:

It consists of single valve mask which diverts exhaled air, blood and bodily fluids away from rescuer. It is used instead of delivering direct mouth-to-mouth ventilation during rescue.
1) Position yourself at victim's side.
2) Place the tip of the pocket mask on victim's bridge of the nose and your index and thumb of one hand placed in 'C' fashion tightly to avoid escape of air.
3) Place the other hand's thumb finger at the bottom end of pocket mask placing it on the edge of victim's chin and lifting the chin forward to provide breaths.
4) While performing, simultaneously observe for victim's chest rise and ROSC.

2) <u>BAG-VALVE-MASK</u>:

It provides positive pressure ventilation to victim who is having problem while breathing.
1) Position yourself at victim's side.
2) Place the mask in 'C' and 'E' fashion of fingers of one hand on victim's bridge of nose and below the edge of chin properly and perform head tilt.
3) Place the tip of the pocket mask on victim's bridge of the nose and your index and thumb of one hand placed in 'C' fashion and the other fingers in 'E' fashion helping victim lift his chin.
4) Squeeze the bag and simultaneously watch for chest rise.
5) If a victim with tracheostomy tube or stoma, then place the mask on top and carry the mentioned steps. Here, in this case, paediatric mask can better work to provide ventilation.

ADULT RECUERS

Number of Rescuer	RESCUER
1	1) Use pocket mask for ventilation 2) Aider to provide chest compressions
2	1) One to provide chest compressions 2) Second can provide ventilations through BVM

CPR COACH

1) Additional Team member who supports High-performance of CPR.
2) Help the compressor provide quality chest compressions.
3) Try to reduce or minimize interruptions to gain maximum output.

CHAPTER 3
BLS FOR CHILD & INFANT

HIGH-QUALITY CPR COMPONENTS – FOR CHILD

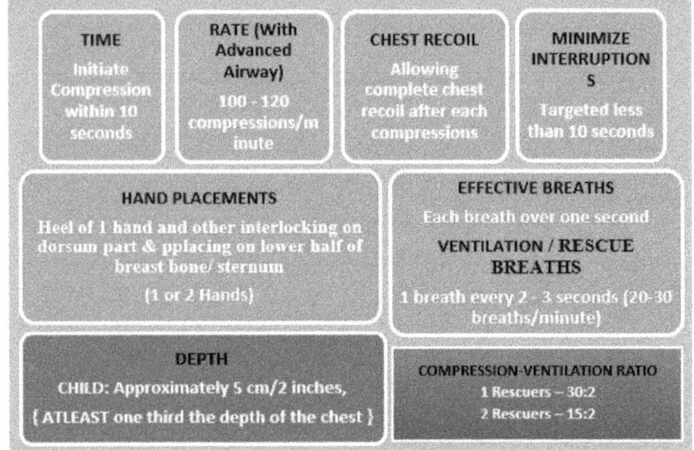

HIGH-QUALITY CPR COMPONENTS – FOR INFANT

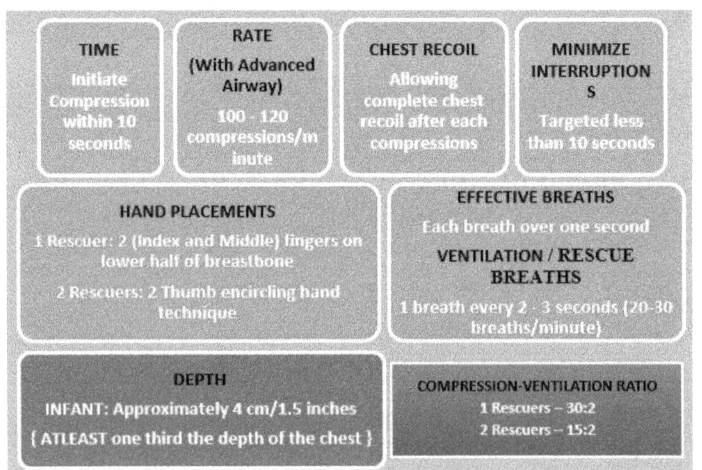

HIGH QUALITY CPR SKILLS: PAEDIATRIC

1) <u>BREATHING:</u>

1) Check for chest rise and fall.
2) Victim's breathing: Monitor until advance help arrives.
3) Victims isn't breathing: Get ready for High-quality CPR.

2) <u>PULSE CHECK:</u>

SITE: Brachial pulse.

1) CHILD: Assess for victim's Trachea, using index and middle finger onto your side.
   Slightly downward between the trachea and muscles of neck, you can feel carotid pulse.
2) INFANT: 2 fingers along inner side of victim's arm, between acromion process and olecranon process.

SIGNS OF POOR PERFUSION

1) Perfusion: Flow of oxygenated blood from heart to overall body tissues.
2) Weak pulse, cool extremities, Loss of consciousness, pale skin and later to cyanosis.

CHEST COMPRESSIONS

Until the heart can be shocked, chest compressions help restore blood flow to the brain and other essential organs, such as the lungs and the heart itself [6].

1) <u>POSITION:</u>

Supine position, on victim's back, flat surface.

2) <u>INTERRUPTIONS:</u>

Lesser the interruptions = Best the outcome.

The ratio of the overall amount of time spent during chest compression to the cumulative time spent for entire resuscitation.

$$CCF = \frac{\text{Total time spent on chest compressions}}{\text{Overall time spent for resuscitation}} * 100$$

At least 60% increase likelihood of survival of ROSC, A good teamwork can achieve 80% survival [7].

PROVIDING BREATHS

Methods of opening airway:

1) HEAD TILT- CHIN LIFT:

1) Placing one hand on victim's forehead and push palm to tilt head back.
2) Placing the other hand fingers below the bony part of chin and lifting it forward.

2) JAW THURST MANEUVER:

This technique is used when the victim has spine, neck injury.
1) Positioning yourself at victim's head end side.
2) Place each of hands on each side of victim's face, and your fingers under the victim's lower jaw and lifting both hands results the jaw forward.

BARRIER DEVICES FOR PROVIDING BREATHS

1) POCKET MASK:

It consists of single valve mask which diverts exhaled air, blood and bodily fluids away from rescuer. It is used instead of delivering direct mouth-to-mouth ventilation during rescue.
1) Position yourself at victim's side.
2) Place the tip of the pocket mask on victim's bridge of the nose and your index and thumb of one hand placed in 'C' fashion tightly to avoid escape of air.
3) Place the other hand's thumb finger at the bottom end of pocket mask placing it on the edge of victim's chin and lifting the chin forward to provide breaths.
4) While performing, simultaneously observe for victim's chest rise and ROSC.

2) <u>BAG-VALVE-MASK:</u>

It provides positive pressure ventilation to victim who is having problem while breathing.
1) Position yourself at victim's side.
2) Place the mask in 'C' and 'E' fashion of fingers of one hand on victim's bridge of nose and below the edge of chin properly and perform head tilt.
3) Place the tip of the pocket mask on victim's bridge of the nose and your index and thumb of one hand placed in 'C' fashion and the other fingers in 'E' fashion helping victim lift his chin.
4) Squeeze the bag and simultaneously watch for chest rise.
5) If a victim with tracheostomy tube or stoma, then place the mask on top and carry the mentioned steps. Here, in this case, paediatric mask can better work to provide ventilation.

ADULT RESCUERS

Number of Rescuer	RESCUER
1	1) Use pocket mask for ventilation 2) Aider to provide chest compressions
2	1) One to provide chest compressions 2) Second can provide ventilations through BVM

CHAPTER 4
ALGORITHM FOR ADULT/ CHILD/ INFANT [9]

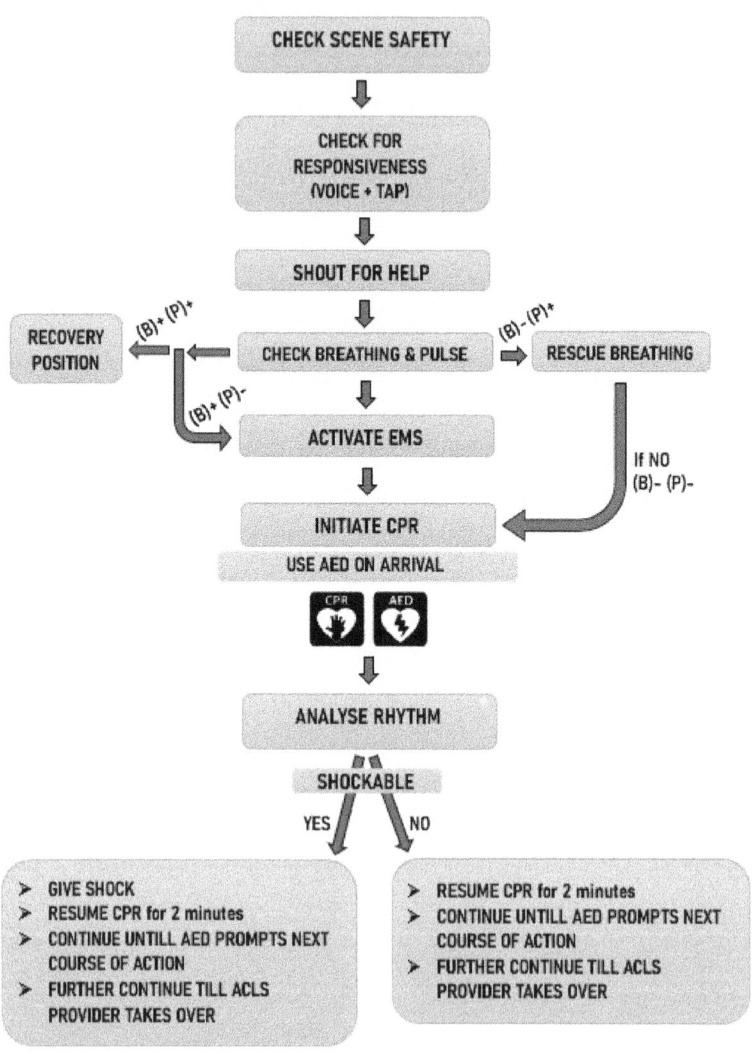

	TAP	PULSE		BREATH	CPR	AED
		UNCONSCIOUS	**CONSCIOUS**			
ADULT	Shoulders	Carotid	Radial	Adult pocket mask / Mouth-to-Mouth	Follow Adult protocol	Attach Adult adhesive pads
CHILD	Shoulders	Carotid	Radial	Paediatric pocket mask / Mouth-to-Mouth	Follow Paediatric protocol	Attach Paediatric adhesive pads
INFANT	Heel of the foot	Brachial	Brachial	Paediatric pocket mask / Mouth-to-Mouth	Follow Paediatric protocol	Attach Paediatric adhesive pads

CHAPTER 5
AED FOR ADULTS & CHILD ≥ 8 YEARS OF AGE

An automated external defibrillator or AED is a small, compact device. When it notices an irregular heartbeat, it corrects it by sending an electric shock through the chest to the heart [10].

DEFIBRILLATION

When an arrhythmia occurs in the lower chambers of your heart, defibrillation is the process of using an electrical current to help your heart return to a normal rhythm.

It is possible to induce ventricular fibrillation and cardiac arrest while defibrillating an individual who does not have ventricular tachycardia or ventricular fibrillation [11].

VF - chaotic electrical activity lacking any recognizable QRS complexes.

pVT - typical broad complex tachycardia, with a heart rate in the range of 100–300 bpm [12].

UNIVERSAL STEPS OF AED

On arrival of AED:
1) Open the cover and POWER ON AED.
2) Follow the instructions prompted by the machine.
3) Attach the adhesive pads to victim's bare chest (One pad onto antero-sternum and other on antero-lateral aspect of victim) (Children: One pad on anterior chest and other on posterior body, just below the midline of scapula).
4) Connect the cables to AED.
5) Stay CLEAR (Very loudly Everybody clear) in order, the machine to analyse the victim's rhythm.
6) If rhythm shockable, then press he charge button and shock the victim and immediately continue CPR + Breaths. If rhythm isn't

shockable, then immediately continue CPR until advance team approaches and transports the victim to Hospital for further treatment.

SPECIAL CONSIDERATIONS

1) Need special attention while attaching AED pads.
2) Hairy skin area on chest: Gently clean the area with easy blade and then attach the AED pads.
3) Presence of fluids: Gently wipe off the area with gauze/pad and then attach the AED pads.
4) Presence of any kind of:
   - Pain medication patch – Slowly remove the transdermal patch, clean the area and then attach the AED pads.
   - Pacemaker/Implants – Avoid applying the AED pads directly on the implants, as the shock can interfere with the electrical impulses generated beneath the skin artificially. You can attach the pads slightly away from the location.
   - Clothing: Respectfully expose the required area only to attach AED pads, as it does not work when placed on clothes or any other material.

MINIMIZE TIMING BETWEEN COMPRESSIONS & SHOCK
DO NOT DELAY CPR AFTER AED

CHAPTER 6
AED FOR CHILDREN < 8 YEARS OF AGE & INFANTS

An automated external defibrillator or AED is a small, compact device. When it notices an irregular heartbeat, it corrects it by sending an electric shock through the chest to the heart [10].

DEFIBRILLATION

FOR INFANTS: Manual defibrillation is mostly preferred to an AED.

When an arrhythmia occurs in the lower chambers of your heart, defibrillation is the process of using an electrical current to help your heart return to a normal rhythm.

It is possible to induce ventricular fibrillation and cardiac arrest while defibrillating an individual who does not have ventricular tachycardia or ventricular fibrillation [11].

VF - chaotic electrical activity lacking any recognizable QRS complexes.

pVT - typical broad complex tachycardia, with a heart rate in the range of 100–300 bpm [12].

UNIVERSAL STEPS OF AED

On arrival of AED:
1) Open the cover and POWER ON AED.
2) Follow the instructions prompted by the machine.
3) Attach the adhesive Paediatric pads to victim's bare chest Antero-posterior (One pad on anterior chest and other on posterior body, just below the midline of scapula).
4) Connect the cables to AED.
5) Stay CLEAR (Very loudly Everybody clear) in order, the machine to analyse the victim's rhythm.

6) If rhythm shockable, then press he charge button and shock the victim and immediately continue CPR + Breaths. If rhythm isn't shockable, then immediately continue CPR until advance team approaches and transports the victim to Hospital for further treatment.

SPECIAL CONSIDERATIONS

1) If Manual defibrillator is not available, then we can use AED equipped with Paediatric dose attenuator is preferred.
2) If this too is not available, then AED without Paediatric dose attenuator can be used [13].

CHAPTER 7
CHOKING

Any foreign body obstruction in upper or lower respiratory tract which may result a victim to choke.

SIGNS OF FOREIGN BODY OBSTRUCTION [14]

Obstruction type	Signs
MILD	Can breathe, cough effectively and speak
SEVERE	Unable to breathe/speak, wheezy sounds, cyanosis, decreasing consciousness

GIVING BREATHS WHILE AIRWAY OBSTRUCTED

1) When victim becomes unconscious, there's chance to worry about because being unconscious, it may relax the muscles present in throat and neck and may be slightly easier to remove the obstacle.
2) While this is under process, chest compression helps wherein it increases the pressure inside which may help the obstacle to be pushed outward.

RELIEF FROM CHOKING IN ADULT/CHILD

1) RESPONSIVE:

1) Abdominal thrusts may help a responsive adult/child free from choking.
2) Standing behind an adult or kneeling behind s child with hands encircling the victim's abdomen, placing hands together.

3) Making your fist by placing thumb outside against victim's abdomen exactly in midline, just below the victim's breastbone and above the navel.
4) By grasping your both hands and pressing forcefully against abdomen inward and in upward direction.
5) On observation, repeat the mentioned steps until the foreign body expels outside.

2) UNRESPONSIVE:

1) Initially, shout for help and try to place the victim slowly flat on ground.
2) If aider gets available, ask him/her to activate emergency response system or call for an ambulance.
3) Immediately start CPR and after 30 or 15 compressions, without checking pulse while reviewing for airway, wide open the victim's mouth and check for the obstacle, if possibly removable by two fingers, then proceed otherwise continue the chest compressions.

RELIEF FROM CHOKING IN INFANT

1) RESPONSIVE:

1) Recommended technique is back slaps and chest thrusts. Avoid abdominal thrust in infant.
2) Aider must be seated comfortable on a chair or kneel if expert.
3) Catch hold the infant in prone position as if facedown. Hold the infant on your hand and by spreading index and middle finger onto infant's cheeks, while by using the heel of other hand to provide 5 forceful back slaps between scapula/shoulder blades pushing in forward direction.
4) After providing back slaps, the current hands must be placed on infant's back along with fingers supporting head and then turn over. The free hand now is used to give chest thrust. 5 chest thrusts just below the nipple line and in middle of chest be given.
5) Repeat until the object ejects outside.

2) <u>UNRESPONSIVE</u>:

1) Initially, shout for help and try to place the infant slowly flat on ground.
2) If aider gets available, ask him/her to activate emergency response system or call for an ambulance.
3) Immediately start CPR and after 30 or 15 compressions, without checking pulse while reviewing for airway, wide open the infant's mouth and check for the obstacle, if possibly removable by two fingers, then proceed otherwise continue the chest compressions.

RELIEF FROM CHOKING IN PREGNANT OR OBESE VICTIMS

Exclusively Chest thrusts to be initiated.

ACTIONS AFTER CHOKING RELIEF

SEEK MEDICAL ATTENTION AFTER EFFECT

CHAPTER 8
MOUTH-TO-MOUTH BREATHING TECHNIQUE

This is taken as separate topic because it is officially not recommended by AHA, if you do not have a Pocket mask or BVM and until the Defibrillation or AED arrives, High-quality chest compressions are recommended.

ADULT, CHILDREN & INFANTS

1) Hold victim's airway with a head tilt-chin lift technique.
2) Pinch victim's nose with thumb and index finger and resting the heel of hand on forehead.
3) After taking long deep breath, seal tight with victim's mouth and release breath, considerably the breath must be delivered over 1 second with a gap of 1 second and then another breath over 1 second.
4) Watch for chest rise simultaneously, if no changes are observed, then repeat the same and even after 2 attempts there is no changes, immediately continue with chest compressions.

CAUTION

GASTRIC INFLATION

CHAPTER 9
TEAM DYNAMICS

Collaborative trained and experienced expert team, which enacts rapidly in a critical situation to save victim's life.

ROLES

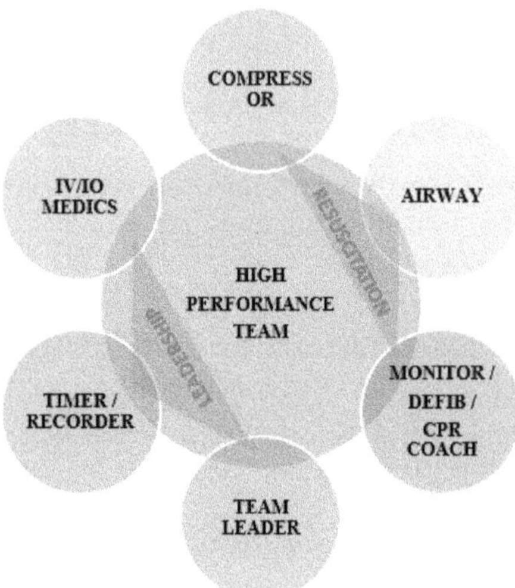

COMPRESSOR: Focuses on high-quality chest compressions.

AIRWAY: Maintains clear airway patency.

MONITOR/ DEFIB/ CPR COACH: Analyse the rhythm, provides ordered shock and CPR Coach; monitors the accuracy, quality of compressions and focuses to minimize interruptions.

TEAM LEADER: Assigns clear tasks to each of High-performance team members & looks overall.

IV/ IO MEDICS: Administers prescribed medications.

TIMER/ RECORDER: Measures the time of chest compressions as well as overall time of resuscitation and calculates CCF.

RESPONSIBILITIES

1) Know your own limitations.
2) Prefer constructive intervention.
3) Knowledge sharing.
4) Summarise and reevaluate.
5) Usage of closed-loop communication.
6) Clear messages.
7) Mutual respect.
8) Coaching and debriefing.

HIGH-PERFORMANCE TEAM [15]

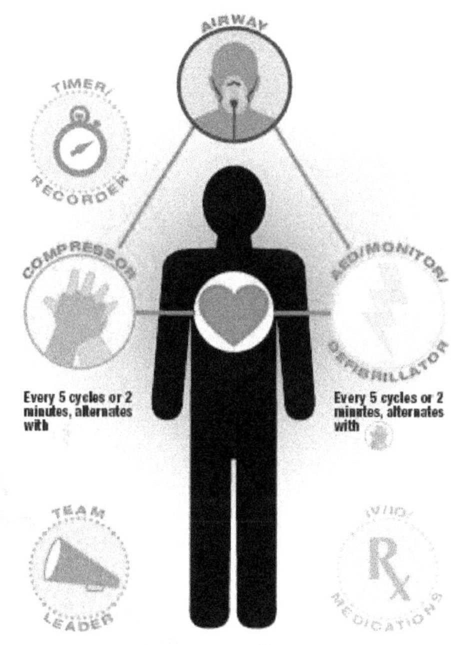

CHAPTER 10
DISTINGUISING LIFE-THREATENING EMERGENCIES

An emergency which is a severe accident or sickness that puts a person's life in danger right now [16].

OPIOIDS

Opioids, also referred to as narcotics, are a family of pharmaceuticals consisting of natural or manufactured substances that interact with nerve cells in an attempt to lessen pain [17].

SIGNS:
Mnemonic: **ABCDS**

A
- Assess Environment for fallen medicinal syrups/tablets/capsules/transdermal patches/syringes

B
- Breathing: Nil/Slow/Shallow along with Blue lips, skin

C
- Choking sounds

D
- Drowsiness

S
- Small pupils

STROKE

A stroke happens when a brain blood artery bursts or when something stops the flow of blood to a certain area of the brain [18].

Mnemonic: **FAST**

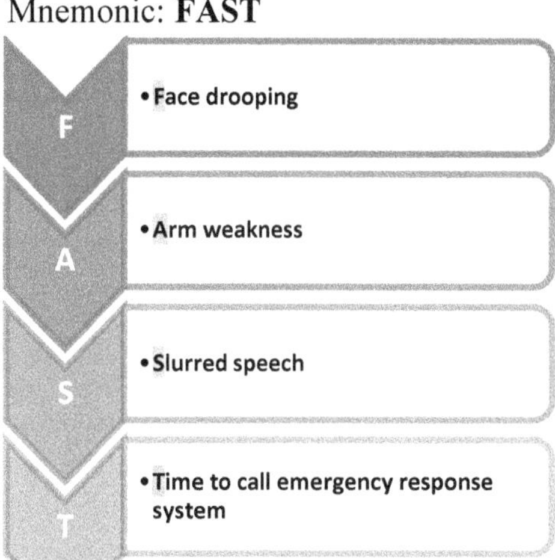

HEART ATTACK

An inadequate supply of blood to a portion of the heart muscle is what causes a heart attack. It is also known as a myocardial infarction [19].

SIGNS:
Mnemonic: **PLAIN**

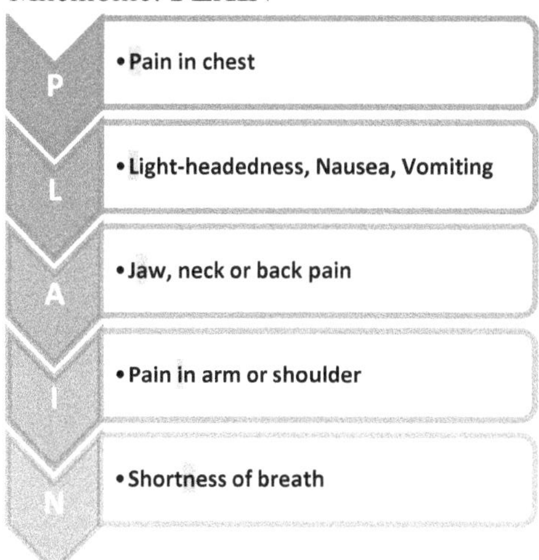

ANAPHYLAXIS

Anaphylaxis is a multi-systemic allergic reaction that is characterized as a broad, quickly growing hypersensitivity reaction that can be extremely dangerous [20].

SIGNS:
Mnemonic:
Mild allergic reaction - **SIR**
Severe allergic reaction - **GA S BREA C**

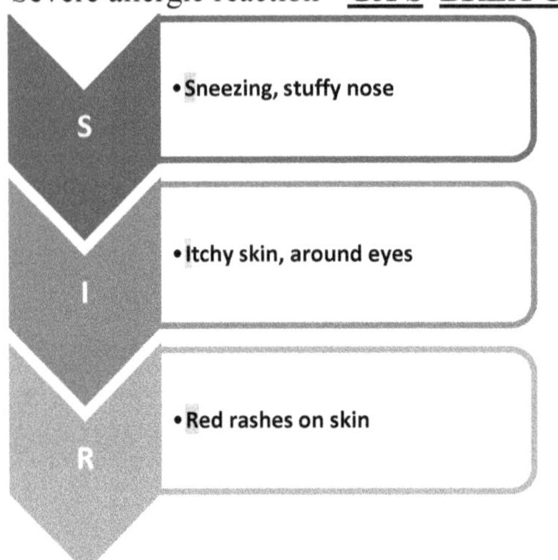

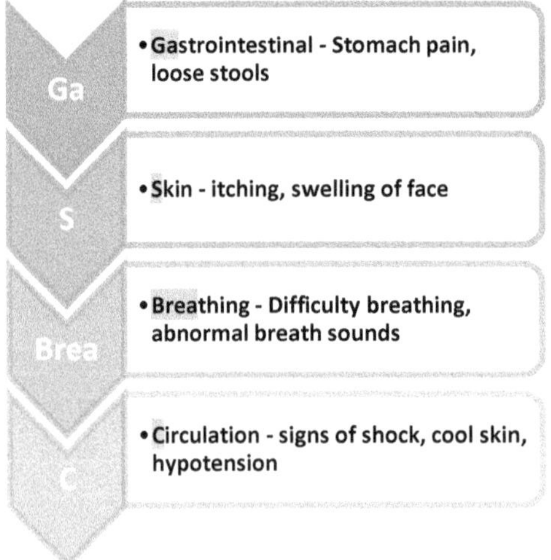

GLOSSARY

1) FIRST RESPONDER: Someone who is in charge of responding quickly to an emergency or accident scene in order to offer aid.
2) DEFIBRILLATION: Giving a transthoracic electrical current to a patient who is suffering from any of these two ventricular dysrhythmias (VT or pVT).
3) RESUSCITATION: the act of pulling someone out of unconsciousness.
4) CARDIAC ARREST: The condition when the heart stops beating unexpectedly and abruptly.
5) LAY RESCUERS: Someone who lacks the professional training to provide better medical care.
6) CHAOTIC: An entirely disorganized and confused state.
7) PACEMAKER: An electronic cardiac support device that regulates the heartbeat for people with specific heart problems by producing rhythmic electrical impulses.
8) THRUSTS: To push forcibly or hardly.
9) NAUSEA: An uneasy sensation at the back of your throat or a queasy feeling in your stomach.
10) VOMITING: An involuntary, forceful discharge of contents from stomach.
11) DROWSINESS: Sensation of feeling sleepy or lazy.
12) BRADYCARDIA: A heartbeat that is lower than usual (< 60 beats per minute).
13) TACHYCARDIA: A heartbeat that is greater than usual (> 100 beats per minute).
14) BRADYPNEA: Abnormal slow breathing.
15) TACHYPNRA: Quick and shallow breathing.
16) HYPOTENSION: An individual's pressure in blood vessels is below 90 / 60 mmHg.
17) HYPERTENSION: An individual's pressure in blood vessels is below 140 / 90 mmHg.

18) HYPOVOLEMIA: A state of low extracellular fluid volume secondary to water loss and sodium.
19) HYPERVOLEMIA: A state of having excess fluid volume retention in an individual's body.

REFERENCES

1. What is BLS? [Internet]. Red Cross. [cited 2024 May 18]. Available from: https://www.redcross.org/take-a-class/performing-bls/what-is-bls

2. Cunningham L. The importance of learning Basic Life Support (BLS) [Internet]. Blue Guard. Blue Guard Middle East; 2022 [cited 2024 May 18]. Available from: https://www.blueguardme.com/blog/the-importance-of-learning-basic-life-support-bls/

3. Topjian AA, Raymond TT, Atkins D, Chan M, Duff JP, Joyner BL Jr, et al. Part 4: Pediatric basic and advanced life support: 2020 American heart association guidelines for cardiopulmonary resuscitation and emergency cardiovascular care. Circulation [Internet]. 2020;142(16_suppl_2). Available from: http://dx.doi.org/10.1161/cir.0000000000000901

4. Panchal AR, Bartos JA, Cabañas JG, Donnino MW, Drennan IR, Hirsch KG, et al. Part 3: Adult basic and advanced life support: 2020 American heart association guidelines for cardiopulmonary resuscitation and emergency cardiovascular care. Circulation [Internet]. 2020;142(16_suppl_2). Available from: http://dx.doi.org/10.1161/cir.0000000000000916

5. Cdc.gov. [cited 2024 May 18]. Available from: https://www.cdc.gov/infectioncontrol/pdf/strive/PPE103-508.pdf

6. Rod Brouhard E-P. How do chest compressions actually work? [Internet]. Verywell Health. 2013 [cited 2024 May 18]. Available from: https://www.verywellhealth.com/how-do-chest-compressions-work-1298428

7. Krishnan S, Mathew D, Abraham S, Varghese S, Thomas M, Palatty B. Chest compression fraction and factors influencing it. J Emerg Trauma Shock [Internet]. 2022 [cited 2024 May 18];15(1):41. Available from: http://dx.doi.org/10.4103/jets.jets_36_21

8. Madden A-M, Meng M-L. Cardiopulmonary resuscitation in the pregnant patient. BJA Educ [Internet]. 2020;20(8):252–8. Available from: http://dx.doi.org/10.1016/j.bjae.2020.03.007

9. Algorithms [Internet]. cpr.heart.org. [cited 2024 May 18]. Available from: https://cpr.heart.org/en/resuscitation-science/cpr-and-ecc-guidelines/algorithms

10. Heart.org. [cited 2024 May 18]. Available from: https://www.heart.org/-/media/files/health-topics/answers-by-heart/what-is-an-aed.pdf

11. Defibrillation [Internet]. Cleveland Clinic. [cited 2024 May 18]. Available from: https://my.clevelandclinic.org/health/treatments/23021-defibrillation

12. Geekymedics.com. [cited 2024 May 18]. Available from: https://geekymedics.com/shockable-vs-non-shockable-rhythms-in-cardiac-arrest/

13. Berg MD, Schexnayder SM, Chameides L, Terry M, Donoghue A, Hickey RW, et al. Part 13: Pediatric basic life support: 2010 American heart association guidelines for cardiopulmonary resuscitation and emergency cardiovascular care. Circulation [Internet]. 2010;122(18_suppl_3). Available from: http://dx.doi.org/10.1161/circulationaha.110.971085

14. Knott L, Colin Tidy M. Choking and foreign body airway obstruction [Internet]. Patient.info. [cited 2024 May 18]. Available from: https://patient.info/doctor/choking-and-foreign-body-airway-obstruction-fbao

15. Amazonaws.com. [cited 2024 May 18]. Available from: https://aclsonline.s3.amazonaws.com/live/cms/image/80a64730ec9d4 4d584b567d1f784ec84/unnamed%20(22).jpg

16. Ramanayake RPJC, Ranasingha S, Lakmini S. Management of emergencies in general practice: Role of general practitioners. J Family Med Prim Care [Internet]. 2014 [cited 2024 May 18];3(4):305. Available from: http://dx.doi.org/10.4103/2249-4863.148089

17. Opioids [Internet]. Cleveland Clinic. [cited 2024 May 18]. Available from: https://my.clevelandclinic.org/health/drugs/21127-opioids

18. CDC. About [Internet]. Stroke. 2024 [cited 2024 May 18]. Available from: https://www.cdc.gov/stroke/about/index.html

19. CDC. About heart attack symptoms, risk, and recovery [Internet].
Heart Disease. 2024 [cited 2024 May 18]. Available from:
https://www.cdc.gov/heart-disease/about/heart-
attack.html?CDC_AAref_Val=https://www.cdc.gov/heartdisease/hear
t_attack.htm

20. McLendon K, Sternard BT. Anaphylaxis. StatPearls Publishing; 2023.

www.ingramcontent.com/pod-product-compliance
Lightning Source LLC
Chambersburg PA
CBHW041649150726
48005CB00015BB/2544